RECALCULATING FOR ENTREPRENEURS

A PRACTICAL ROADMAP FOR DECISIONS THAT MATTER

Ilana Krause and Lee Krause

Recalculating for Entrepreneurs:
A Practical Roadmap for Decisions that Matter

Printed in the United States of America

For permissions, bulk orders, or bookings, please address correspondence to: ineed2recalculate@gmail.com

ISBN: 979-8-9854146-0-8

Preface — The Story of Recalculating

My father always has the best advice. At age 14, I had a notes section in my cell phone where I would write down all the wise ideas he had told me that helped guide me or get me through a hard time. He always seemed to have sage advice for any sort of problem that came up.

I became a sort of collector of such advice, not only from my father but from myriad sources I encountered. I would take these bits and pieces of great counsel and use them to advise my friends. They were always impressed with my wisdom, but I give credit to all the wise people whose advice I acquired.

Inspired by this acquired wisdom, I developed a driving passion in high school and college to help people become better critical thinkers and problem solvers. I created a community outreach team in high school that helped underserved students learn a six-step critical thinking process. This process was taught as part of the Future Problem-Solving Program, a grade school program that stimulates critical and creative thinking skills. In college, I conducted academic research for five years on how to develop curricula to help engineering students become better problem solvers and be better prepared to tackle real-world, open-ended problems.

Every time I came home from a break at college, my father and I would go for a run. We would talk through different situations my friends were in and think about how their decision processes could be improved. There always was so much to learn from each situation. For example, my father taught me not to make a final decision until you have to, as you want to get the maximum amount of information to inform your decision-making process. This was a key insight when making my graduate school decision, where I learned last-minute that the professor I wanted to work for didn't have the anticipated funding, so it made more sense to start in the industry. I started applying all the methodological critical thinking strategies I was learning to help bolster my own ability to make quicker, smarter long-term decisions.

On one of our runs, we came up with the idea of writing a book about all these decision-making ideas to help people gain the critical thinking skills needed to become better decision-makers.

Over the course of my last two years of college, we carved out time to interview top decision-makers, those who would be considered "most improved" in their decision-making process. Additionally, we interviewed people with unique stories that could help others gain insight into becoming better decision-makers and critical thinkers. Their stories taught us more about the process of leveraging critical thinking skills to mitigate risk, using and identifying skills/experiences to take advantage of opportunities, and the ratio of people planning their journey vs. letting the course run its path. Their stories, bolstered by both personal and experience-based research, are the basis for Recalculating and the foundation for *Recalculating for Entrepreneurs*.

Table of Contents

5. **Adjust Your Speed**

- Reach out to companies and people with a perspective on the "riskiness" of the opportunity
- What are the drivers that apply to companies vs. a startup vs. creating your own company?
- Get in touch with how comfortable and interested you are in risk when seeking opportunities

6. **Dealing with Roadblocks**

- How to bounce back from "no" responses or rejections

7. **Active Thinking Along the Route**

- What feedback are you receiving during this process, and how does this impact you?
- How to continue to build your network to support your career

Intro and Background

Whether you are searching for your dream job, launching a new business, or trying to figure out your next opportunity, there are certain steps you can take to set yourself up for success. These steps are key in understanding what your goals are and what you need to do to help achieve them, and they can be learned with the help of *Recalculating for Entrepreneurs* and *The Entrepreneur's Resume*. *Recalculating for Entrepreneurs* provides the foundation to develop your personal brand and know what goals you want to achieve. *The Entrepreneur's Resume* helps you take those learnings into action so you can secure the opportunity of your dreams.

This content builds your critical thinking skills, decision-making abilities, goal setting approaches, and career planning strategies to make you competitive on the job market and successful in achieving your short- and long-term goals. These concepts are relevant to anyone and everyone who wants to enjoy life's journey and become a better decision-maker, critical thinker, and self-marketer. We all are our own CEOs and should start to think about decision-making and goal setting in that way. You do not need to be a founder to find this content relevant. You just need to be open-minded about improving your performance and your current methods to achieve your goals.

We have proven that this content helps set you up for long-term fulfillment both personally and professionally. From identifying your personal strengths, filtering through short/long terms goals, to getting the job offer you have always dreamed of, this interactive content is here to set you up for success. Start thinking about your life from the lens of an entrepreneur and see how this mindset magnifies what you can achieve.

Chapter One: What's in Your Backpack?

In this chapter, you will learn:

- What skills do you bring to the table?
- How to identify your unique contributions and the value you add
- What experiences do you have that make you a competitive candidate?
- Are there any gaps to fill that can be done quickly?

Have You Ever Felt Lost?

People commonly feel overwhelmed and frozen during uncertain times in life. How are you supposed to know the right decision to make? For example: What company to start? What job to accept? What city to move to? What career path to follow? What are the steps needed to achieve my goals? Sometimes, there is so much going on, the easiest thing to do is to put off the decision or ignore the situation altogether and let fate take control.

If you struggle when it comes to making life choices, you are like most people, who make even the biggest decisions based on intuition or emotion — a hit-or-miss proposition at best.

There is a better way: There is a way to think about decision-making that allows you to examine your goals and make decisions that are aligned with your desired end destination. With due diligence to understand your skills and experiences, you are setting yourself up for long-term success toward achieving your goals. This process is the foundation for helping you identify your ideal job and help you actualize your dreams. For entrepreneurs, you are constantly pitching yourself, your ideas, and your business. To do that successfully, you need to understand how your skills and experiences have made you uniquely suitable for the job. This can be broken down by analyzing what is in your backpack, which is filled with your toolbox of skills and journal of experiences.

What's in Your Backpack?

For your journey, you will need a backpack. This metaphorical backpack is filled with your toolbox of skills you will have developed, along with your journal of life's experiences. You always have access to your backpack. It helps you stay prepared, informed, and on the right track during your journey. On your journey, you are constantly acquiring more experiences resulting from both good and bad decisions. Store them in your backpack so you can access them at any point in time. These experiences will help inform future decisions.

Recalculating for Entrepreneurs gives you the tools to figure out your destination, how best to get there, and how to handle surprises on your journey. It helps you develop a clear decision path and equips you with tools to guide you through confusing and unexpected experiences.

Think of making changes in your decision-making skills as a pilot making small changes in the trajectory of an airplane. It will make a huge difference over time in where the airplane eventually lands. It is much harder to make large course changes once you arrive at the destination. By the time you realize your planned destination, it is not where you want to be, and it is difficult to change trajectory.

Skills you place in your toolbox and life experiences documented in your journal both contribute to your backpack.

What's in Your Toolbox?

Your toolbox is comprised of your skills, whether natural or learned, obtained from degrees, training, certificates, etc. Everyone has a toolbox of skills, and there are probably more in your toolbox than you realize. Take an inventory of all the tools you have. Be honest in evaluating your skill set, as it is crucial to think about the skills in your toolbox as you get started. Toolbox assessment may help you decide where you want to go and what goals you want to achieve along the way.

Once you understand your foundational skills, a clear path may arise, or you may realize the gaps in skills you will need to fill in to achieve your goals. If it is difficult to begin with specific skills, start thinking about things you enjoy doing, and link those to skills you have developed through the process. What are some things you are good at? What do you enjoy doing? What do people come to you for help with? Examples of this examination of skills are shown below. At the end of the chapter, there is a blank chart you can complete. It is extremely helpful to see this all written out, as opposed to keeping it in your head.

What skills do I have?	Where did I acquire that skill?
Communication	School
Organization	My mom
Strong math ability	Calculus class
How to read a balance sheet	Business minor
Knowledge about material properties/testing procedures	B.S. in Materials Engineering
Ability to work with small children	Red Cross babysitting certification
Problem-solving	Future Problem-Solving Program, 6-step Critical Thinking Process
Relaxation	Yoga classes at the gym + meditation app
Graphic design	Online class in high school
Cooking	Guidance from Grandma + YouTube videos
Tech-savvy	Digital native

Some things that may be in your toolbox:

- Communicates well with others
- Creative thinking
- Language skills
- Works well with people
- Emotional intelligence

- Quick reaction times
- Attention to details
- Marketing skills
- Programming skills
- Website development
- Certifications
- Photography
- Graphic design
- Product development
- Skills learned from your major
- Skills picked up from different jobs
- How to raise capital
- Finance/accounting skills
- Understanding contracts
- Negotiation skills
- Closing deals (sales, business, etc.)

When thinking about your toolbox from an entrepreneurial view, be sure to stay open-minded regarding the skills you have identified. The world can benefit from the many non-traditional skills that contribute to your being a unique individual with a unique skill set. Examples of this are skills that are not expected within your industry, such as strong creative design or communication skills within a technical role. **Take a moment to fill out your toolbox below.**

What skills do I have?	Where did I acquire that skill?	How does this relate to your goals?

It is important to recognize that this toolbox will be stored in your backpack during your journey. At every experience and situation you encounter, take note of what you have learned and keep this knowledge accessible in your backpack. As long as you are able to garner something from every situation you experience – learning from both good and bad experiences – you still are gathering tools to add to your backpack. They will help you later on your journey. Remember, you always have your backpack on, and you cannot lose the skills and knowledge you have acquired.

Some say luck is the intersection of preparation and opportunity. Your backpack provides you with preparation from past experiences and the ability to recognize when an opportunity arises on your journey. With this mindset, you will be able to take advantage of a greater percentage of opportunities.

What About Your Journal?

Your journal documents all your experiences and interactions from which you have learned (your likes, dislikes, strengths, etc.). You can keep a physical journal if you prefer to write things down. It is a running list in which you keep track of all your valued experiences. It is more than a resume, as it also includes realizations you have had along the way.

Your backpack encompasses your toolbox and adventure journal and is something that is always accessible during your journey. Take a moment to review this example journal before filling in your own. Remember that this is a living document in which you accumulate experiences to help shape your path forward.

Experience I had	What I learned from it
Managing a product development team	The importance of communicating long-term goals and purpose to motivate the team. Products rely on a brand to set them up for success.
Starting my own t-shirt company	Maintaining inventory and marketing are key pillars to success. You cannot compete against your supplier.
Summer research experience	I hated being in a lab all day with minimal contact with people other than my graduate student.
Being mentored by Dr. R	That I was more prepared for my courses than I thought, and that I underestimated my ability to solve problems.
Summer internship	I really like the fast-moving pace of business, and I am good at making technical presentations.
Getting rejected from all internship positions, applying to research positions instead, and getting into a great summer program	That sometimes you can do all the right things, and it comes down to a matter of chance to achieve the goals you put effort towards.

This physical list is more likely to help you visualize your big picture. **Take a moment to fill in your journal, and be sure to continue to update it as new experiences arise that shape you.**

Experience I had	What I learned from it

Needing That Extra Boost

It is true that, for many situations, you can navigate to your destination just by leveraging the life experiences you have. However, there will be some cases where you need a more formalized set of skills to travel the path you want to go down. Along your journey, you must realize when you need to pivot to get an extra boost.

Sometimes, you can achieve your career goal without earning additional academic degrees. Other times, you cannot ascend to the next level without supplementary training. It is important to understand the reality of your barriers early in your career. Are you able to talk to advisors in the field to determine whether higher education is needed as a barrier buster? How does it impact your pay or promotion prospects? Take some time to explore the landscape. Use your network to connect with people in a company/role in which you are interested. Some key questions to ask as a starting point are:

- Walk me through your career journey... how did you get to where you are now?
- Did you feel you needed higher-level degrees to achieve your current position?
- Is this the position you always dreamed of having?
- What are your career goals, and how have they changed over time?
- Knowing what you know now, what would you have done differently in your career?
- Tell me about a time you felt there was a barrier to your career growth?

What are other questions that come to mind to begin asking?

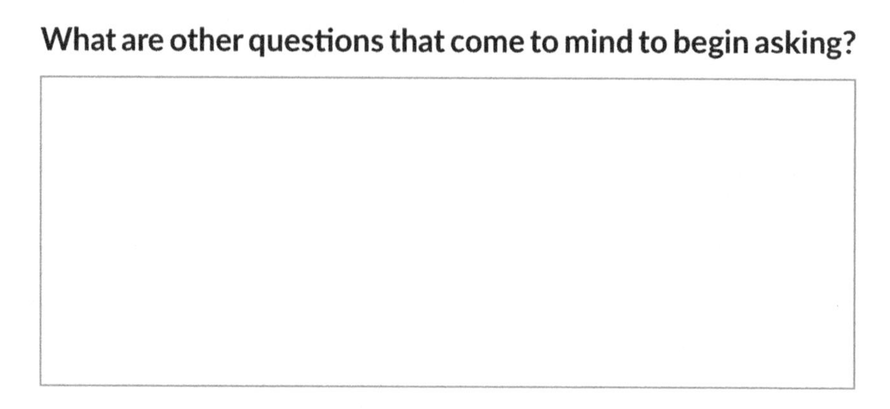

If you are unable to organize a conversation with someone in a future position you think you may be interested in, think about different ways to learn about what is necessary. Look at LinkedIn profiles on individuals who are performing roles in which you are interested ... what type of background and education do they have? You can learn a lot about timing and what may be necessary by doing background research like this. Weighing these factors will help you understand which route may be best.

Choosing Between Paved and Dirt Roads

There are two choices when deciding how to connect your backpack to your overall destination:

1) **The paved road** – This is the road to take when pursuing what comes easily to you, to access the tools you already have. For example: math and memorization both come easily to you. You see it and remember it, and putting things together is a snap. So, you are going to pursue a goal directly related to these skills.

2) **The dirt road that is still being created** – This is the road to take if you want to pursue what doesn't

necessarily come easily to you. You feel passionate about pursuing it, and you are motivated to overcome obstacles to reach your goal. For example: math is difficult, but you enjoy persevering and figuring things out. So, you start reading books on math and watching videos online. You join the math team. This is where time and resources come into play. You will put in the time and leverage all the resources you have to make this path work.

Neither path is more correct, more impressive, or more rewarding than the other. It is all about how you perceive each path and what appeals to you. It depends on what type of journey you want to take.

Getting in Touch

Is it hard for you to identify what skills you have or what qualities stand out? Sometimes, you need to take a couple of minutes to write out your thoughts and ideas to truly understand your strengths and weaknesses. Think about frequent compliments you receive and how that relates to a specific skill or ability. You can ask friends, family, and co-workers to contribute ideas to this diagram. Sometimes, others know you better than yourself. **Map out these qualities below.**

Frequent compliments or things people come to you for	What skill does this correlate to?

Here are some questions to think about as you begin to document your strengths:

- What do my friends/family come to me to help them with?
- What are things that I like to do that do not feel like work?
- What type of jobs do I lean towards doing when I have the option?

Understanding your strengths is the key to building and capitalizing on them. Understanding what is in your backpack enables you to constantly learn from experiences and apply them to help achieve your goals. This serves as your foundation during your journey to help you achieve your goals and continue growing and developing in meaningful and relevant ways.

Chapter Two: Be Your Own Navigator

In this chapter, you will learn:

- How to take charge of your destiny—Sometimes, you need to push the limits of established plans if you want to achieve a specific outcome.
- How to understand people's biases—If you can understand people's perspectives, you can effectively filter through advice.
- How to move forward (and not look back). When you make big decisions, think carefully, understand the situation, and make the best decision you can at that time. Once you make your decision, stick with it.
- How to understand how to sell your brand based on where you want to go.
- How to identify what is important to you and areas where you are willing to be flexible.

Being your own navigator is hard and can feel painful and overwhelming. This can happen if you are thrust into a situation due to circumstances outside of your control. It can happen if you are pushed into making decisions for which you feel ill-prepared. And it can happen if you are riddled with self-doubt and fear that your decision will be random and haphazard, leading to a poor outcome. As an entrepreneur, there are two critical skills that directly support being your own navigator:

1. Belief in your brand.

Your brand refers to your values, work ethic, personality, vision for the future, and so on. It is how you are represented and what you are pitching in conjunction with your business or idea. Believing in your brand means you have confidence in yourself and your ability to make decisions.

2. Confidence in yourself that you can get the job done.

This is critical when selling yourself during an interview or pitching your business idea to potential investors. Confidence that you are the right person to do the job is crucial. You gain this confidence in many ways (remember your backpack). This includes understanding your strengths and weakness, wisdom gained from past experiences, and having a support network of people who can help.

All these components are the building blocks required to navigate your journey.

Three Types of Navigators

Being your own navigator is hard. Whether you are thrust into the situation due to circumstances outside of your control or gradually pushed out of the nest to make a decision on your own, it can be difficult to take control of your decision-making. However it happens, it may feel painful and overwhelming. You may be riddled with self-doubt or feel you are ill-prepared to make hard decisions if your decision-making process is haphazard, which could endanger your plans for your long-term goals.

After interviewing a wide range of individuals, we have come up with three broad categories of navigator types. Keep in mind that a combination of characteristics from different categories is normal, and there really is no one right style. You are encouraged to identify one of the navigation styles that seems the best fit. Then you can directly apply the decision-making skills as outlined in that style. Keep in mind, your navigation style may change over time, and it may be a combination of styles.

1. **Planners** – As its name implies, these are the people who take the time to plan out their journey and have a clear goal. For example: You want to be a Biomedical Engineer and develop cures for major illnesses that have impacted friends and family. You want to start a company in the cryptocurrency space, and so on. Remember, planners have a clear goal and have mapped out steps to achieve their goal. A few key areas that planners should consider when making decisions:
    a. Take an inventory of the tools and experiences you have accumulated in life.
    b. Be honest in evaluating your skill set – and then formulate a plan to acquire any missing skills and experiences you need to succeed.
    c. It is appropriate to take shortcuts to achieve your goals. It is OK to make minor changes to your plan. For example, if an unexpected opportunity arises, do not immediately rule it out. It could be a shortcut to your goal.

2. **Explorers** – For explorers, you need to explore your world. Whether it is traveling or working a variety of jobs, you may feel lost or crave the excitement of the unknown. Exploring allows you to discover what you enjoy and gain experience along the way. It helps you become a well-rounded individual who is a jack of all trades. Keep in

mind; there are many routes to a destination. Some key points to consider when making decisions:

a. Be aware and keep track of the experiences (both successes and failures) during your journey. This is the reason you are exploring.

b. As you explore, leverage your backpack to the maximum extent possible. Make sure your core skills are mastered and know how to apply them.

c. Be willing to change course as required.

d. Once you find your passion, pursue it.

3. **Drivers** – These are navigators who have a broad objective or passion: "I want to save the environment." "I want to be rich." "I want to focus on my spiritual life." This broad passion defines a general direction for your journey. You do not have a route planned, but you have a direction and a broad goal. If you want to save the world, you can become an environmental lawyer and focus on public policy, a material engineer and develop zero waste products, or an activist trying to focus awareness on an issue. There are many routes to achieve your goals based on overarching principles. When decision making, drivers should consider:

   a. Your tools should align with your guiding principles.

   b. It is essential to understand the tools that best serve you and leverage them on your journey.

   c. Stay open-minded towards different paths that lead to the same goals.

   d. Look for mentors outside your inner circle who have similar goals to yours. Do not over-index advisors in one specific area.

What type of navigator style(s) do you identify with and why?

In each of the future chapters, we provide a few concepts you should carry with you regarding your decision-making style. For this chapter, "Be Your Own Navigator," the key concept is that you are the ultimate decision-maker. While trusted advisors provide advice and opinions, ultimately, you need to take ownership of your decisions. For each of the decision-making styles, we have compiled ideas for finding and utilizing advisors. We examine these concepts in more depth later, but it is important to keep them in mind moving forward.

1. **Planners** – Get diversified viewpoints from people in the field. Quickly analyze the information, make the decision, and move on. Learn from the experience to improve future decisions.

2. **Explorers** – Seek individuals who are active in the fields in which you are interested. Use this to better understand where your passion or ideal fit is.

3. **Drivers** – Look for advisors who have achieved multiple successes in similar fields. This ensures you are connecting

with people who understand what it takes to achieve your goals from multiple angles.

The clearer the goals, the easier decision-making gets. The more you practice decision-making, and the more you know about yourself, the quicker you will get good at the decision-making process.

Do you feel you are getting the right type of advisors per your navigator type? Why or why not? What type of advisor should you be looking for moving forward?

What It Takes to Be Your Own Navigator

What does it take to be your own navigator? This question can be broken down into a few major concepts covered in this chapter. A critical aspect is self-efficacy, which is the belief that you will be successful. An integral component of being your own navigator is learning to take ownership of your decisions. Taking ownership means that you are in control and are responsible for the outcome, for monitoring the decision, and taking corrective action as required — also known as "recalculation." Most importantly, it means learning from both success and failures. Each experience can be leveraged in the future to improve your decision-making ability.

Self-efficacy: One of the most important tools you have available is something many people take for granted. It is something that people either build up or break down, and it is something that seeps into everyone's story, both success, and failure.

Psychologist Albert Bandura defined self-efficacy as the belief in one's ability to succeed in specific situations or accomplish a task. Self-efficacy plays a significant role in determining how we achieve goals, approach challenges, and accomplish tasks. Without it, we would continually seek external validation every step of every journey. Self-efficacy is acquired over time as a result of mastering tasks and compliments from others. When we accomplish something, our perception of our ability increases dramatically, and so does our self-efficacy. When someone praises our work, we believe we are competent in that area, increasing our self-efficacy.

This tool is vital because self-efficacy is both an evaluation and perception of ourselves. Many times, our self-efficacy beliefs and our ability level do not match. This is when problems in decision-making occur. Part of assessing your toolbox is evaluating your self-efficacy regarding decision-making. Do you make decisions but constantly question your choice? If you make a decision but a friend questions your judgment, do you immediately shift your view to agree with your friend on your misstep? Why is it that we can so easily reroute decisions based on minor external influences? It all leads back to self-efficacy.

In decision-making, you must always trust your instincts and thought processes. Believe in your abilities to make rational and beneficial decisions by utilizing processes in the upcoming chapters and trusting your gut.

Last Minute or Just in Time?

Your goal is to make the best decision in the least amount of time. Based on the information you have, what is the best decision you can make quickly? Is there additional information that is worth waiting for that would alter your decision? As you master using critical thinking to drive decision-making, you will notice you can quickly make high-quality decisions in familiar areas – that is, in areas where you have the domain understanding and background to support the decision. For areas that are uncharted, you will rely on processing new information and advice from advisors to arrive at a decision.

A key component of learning from your successes and failures is answering the questions "When did I have enough information to make the decision?" and "What went right or wrong that would have changed the outcome?" It is not enough to understand how to improve your decision scaffolding. It is also imperative to improve the speed at which quality decisions are made. Finding the balance between making quick decisions and quality decisions is key.

Do not be afraid to make a decision, and once it is made, move forward quickly. If it becomes apparent that it is the wrong decision, figure out a plan to recalculate or select a new destination. Learn from both good and bad decisions. You are the final decision-maker, but that does not mean you need to make decisions alone. You have advisors who can help based on their past experiences. During your journey, beware of over-bias in your decision-making. This can be either your own internal bias or bias that comes from advisors with an agenda who are trying to influence your decision process.

My father prided himself on the creed of "I don't make a decision until I have enough information to make the decision or am forced to make a decision based on a deadline." Granted, it drove my mother crazy because decisions would be made at the last minute. But it enabled my father to make the most informed decision possible.

You usually have control over your decision-making timeline. Keep that in mind when external forces try to pressure you onto a path earlier than you feel ready. There will be times when you might need or want additional information to make the decision. You are in the driver's seat, and you control your speed. Once you begin to make decisions, do some reflection: Did I have enough information to decide at an earlier point in time? How could I have optimized the speed of this process? These types of questions will strengthen your decision-making scaffold and prepare you to make more effective and efficient decisions in the future.

Reflect on a time you made a decision that took longer than you expected it to take. Looking back on it, when did you feel like you had enough information to make the same decision?

What was the decision about?

Did I have enough information to decide at an earlier point in time?

How could I have optimized the speed of this process?

What to Remember

It is your life. Sometimes other people try to influence it. Ultimately, you have the final say and the final vision for what you want your life to be. Honestly, it was nice to be reminded of that simple fact at multiple points during my decision-making process. Many friends struggled with this concept when trying to decide on job offers. For many, families put pressure on them to accept jobs closer to home, regardless of how the opportunity measured up against other offers in terms of pay, work conditions, and enjoyment. If you value family, proximity to your loved ones is going to affect your scaffolding. However, you can still support your family without being in the same state. If you get a higher-paying job out of state, you could still support them and visit often. There are many ways priorities in scaffolding can manifest themselves. But your decisions should be based on you first, and then other factors. It is your life, and you are going to be the one who lives it.

In life, there comes a time when we become our own navigators. We will receive guidance from both wanted and unwanted sources. The hard part is understanding biases and filtering through the information to make an informed decision aligned with our goals and priorities. How can we form our own decisions when bombarded with information from others with all types of viewpoints? The key lies in self-efficacy. Believe that you can make your own decisions and use information from others to guide your thought process, but not to make the final decision. Be aware of the biases that influence the advice you are receiving. This helps you piece together relevant components to inform your decision.

Once you make your decision, do not look back. When you make big decisions, think carefully, understand the situation, and make the best decision that you can at that time. Then avoid second-guessing yourself.

Chapter Three: Figuring Out Your Destination

In this chapter, you will learn:

- What companies are you interested in and why? What do you value most in a job/opportunity you are exploring?
- How does this contribute to long-term career goals?
- Create a matrix for evaluating goals
- How do these align with your skills and experiences?

GPS apps are not helpful without a destination. In some cases, figuring out where you want to go is the most challenging part. As so, many destinations seem appealing and intriguing. How are you supposed to narrow down where you want to end up? How can you distinguish between destinations that seem great vs. destinations that are best for you? For some, the thought of having to choose is too much. So, they start driving in hopes that, one day, either they figure out where they genuinely want to go or end up somewhere they are happy.

You Want to Go Where?

The destination can be viewed in many ways based on someone's current situation and age. In talking to several people during our journey in putting *Recalculating* together, it was interesting to hear how many individuals did not feel they had a destination. But as we spoke, it became apparent their destination was not a single location. We expected to hear, "I want to be the CEO of the next big thing" or "I want to be a veterinarian for horses." Instead, we heard, "I want to be the best at corporate law but stick to my principles on being compassionate to others." Money was not the most important factor for many people, although it was important to maintain a certain lifestyle.

Another popular response was, "I didn't have a destination, but I had guiding principles that acted as the destination." These included: "I want to earn enough to support my lifestyle," "I want to make industries and products more sustainable," and "I want to help people." This chapter will help you gain a better idea of the type of destination in which you are interested.

One major point is that your destination can change. For some, it can be a stretch goal; for others, a set of steppingstones. There may be new tools or experiences along the journey that alter the destination. All these outcomes along the journey, expected and unexpected, are great. For example, suppose part of your destination was to be financially secure for your retirement, and you have achieved that. In that case, you may update your destination to helping others or creating a legacy through philanthropy.

Timing can be everything. Keep in mind, when an opportunity arises, it is OK to capitalize on it.

Where Do I Even Start?

Before you start the journey, you need to set the destination. It can be extremely broad. For example, your destination may be: "I want to live in the Northwest." It may be specific: "I want to work for Amazon in Seattle as a mechanical engineer in the refrigeration division." Before you set your destination, you need to set as many big-picture goals as possible to ensure you reach your destination. If your destination is

California, going to New York and then figuring out how to get to California will require a lot of recalculating.

Think about the following questions and how they relate to your long-term goals.

- What companies are you interested in and why?
- What do you value most in a job/opportunity you are exploring?
- Are there different life stages where you want to take more or less risk?
- How does this fit in with long-term goals (career, family, health, wealth, etc.)?

Now think about some of the goals you have. Below are some examples of big-pictures goals related to the following categories. **See if you can begin to populate this chart with relevant goals that come to the top of your mind. Think about goals you have achieved and goals you are pursuing.** Continue to update this as your goals change over time. Start thinking about how the goals you have achieved prepare you for your future.

	Goals I have Achieved	Goals I want to Achieve	On a scale of 1-5, how important is this goal to you? (5 = most important)
Career (role, type, company, benefits)			
Location			
Wealth (retirement goals, purchasing larger assets, investing)			
Health			
Family (priority, proximity)			
Education			
Other			

Guiding Principles

The notion of a destination can be overwhelming, and sometimes it can be hard to figure out which steps will lead you to your destination. You may be deciding what internships to apply for or accept. Whether you want to risk starting a new business instead of working for an established company, it is hard to say with certainty what your final destination will be and then plan and execute that journey. However, leveraging the skills and experiences in your backpack are a key component of your journey. By setting a destination, you are selecting a journey that interests you and allows you to find joy along the way. Some people will take the expressway and reach their destination quickly, while others will take the scenic route and accumulate experiences that will serve them well.

Below are examples of guiding principles for different types of navigators:

1. **PLANNERS: Guiding principles to achieve a specific goal to lead a happy, productive, life**

   Career-Related

   - I want to work in the legal field
   - I want to teach others
   - I want to help others through medicine
   - I want to run my own company
   - I want to be a CEO
   - I want to make a lot of money, so I do not have to work
   - I want to invent new things
   - I want to explore the galaxy

Life-Related

- Finding a soul mate
- Writing a book
- Traveling the world

2. **EXPLORERS: Guiding principles during exploration**
    - I want to live in a big city (explore what types of jobs in that city)
    - I am interested in the healthcare industry (e.g., a registered nurse, lab technician, doctor)
    - I really like biology (major in biology, explore related fields)
    - I want to help others (explore the military, Peace Corps, NGO, faith-based organizations)
3. **DRIVERS: Guiding principles that will help you lead a happy, productive life**
    - Being close to my family
    - Helping others rise from adversity
    - Acquiring knowledge
    - Involvement in my faith
    - Taking care of my family
    - Earning a living

What are some driving principles you want to live by? How does that align with your navigator type?

Making the Hop

When you have achieved a goal and are looking ahead to the next goal, is there a gap in the path between where you are now and where you want to go? Bridging gaps between short to medium or medium to long-term goals in actionable ways is what we call "the hop."

Think about hops you may need to make — think about your goals beyond applying to specific jobs.

- What do you want to do, and how can you set yourself up for that?
- What type of work are you seeking, short-term vs. long-term?
- If you need more information to gain clarity, who among your advisors can help directly or utilize their network to help get you the information you need?
- Specifically, what information do you need?

Answering these questions will help you get the information you need to make informed decisions about the next steps to reach your goals.

As you are developing or recalculating your journey, visualize it as hopping between short goals on your way to reaching long-term goals. As you travel, new opportunities will appear, or roadblocks may pop up that you need to navigate around. Later chapters cover how to handle the unknown. In this chapter, we start by breaking down goals into manageable steps.

1. Start by looking at all the tools in your backpack. What are your strengths that help build towards where you want to go?

2. Write down your lofty long-term goal — your dream big.

3. What is some information that would help specify what it will take to get to your goal? What mentors could you ask to gain clarity and information?

4. Now think about the smaller stepping stones between you and your goal. Break down the steps toward your goal below.

1.

2.

3.

4.

For example, if your goal is to be CEO of a Fortune 500 company, what are the steps, the smaller goals, between you and your larger goal?

1) Start a company
2) Sell the company to a major corporation
3) Work at the company to develop new business
4) Switch into finance to improve the corporation
5) Get experience in mergers and acquisitions
6) Become the COO of a company
7) Become the CEO of a company

These are some pretty broad goals. Let's repeat this exercise to get some more granularity on the first step of "Start a company" with varying levels of details on the supporting goals. This gives you a perspective on the different levels of detail that can help you better understand how your larger goals break down into achievable steps.

1. Start a company

- Business Opportunity Analysis
    - Develop Business plan
        - What is the problem I am trying to solve?
            - Customer need/ Pain point being solved
        - What is the solution to the problem (your idea to make money)
            - Develop Minimum Viable Product
        - Size of the market
            - Prove customers will pay for the product
        - Who are your Competitor's

- What differentiates your product
- How are going to make money and how much money can you make?
- How much capital is needed?
- What the funds will be used for?
- How will you use the experience of the Leadership Team
  - Advisory Board - who is on it and what do they bring to the table

- Build Minimum Viable Product
  - Consumer testing of product or concept
  - Manufacturing proof of concept

The example above shows the importance of breaking down lofty goals into manageable actions. When identifying the steps to achieve your goals, consider a variety of sources. This means reaching out to your network to learn from those who had a similar path, using the Internet to your advantage to learn what the typical next steps are, and leveraging mentors who can give you an insider view. Learning from others' journeys — such as mentors who have done similar things — will help ensure you are on the right track when breaking down your larger goals into manageable steps.

Creating Your Pitch Deck

Now start thinking about decision making as pitching an idea to yourself and others through a pitch deck. This is something entrepreneurs do when starting a company from an idea. Pitch decks are evidence of why the idea is great. It helps get others excited about the idea. It helps to raise funds, recruit talent, and is the foundation for developing a business plan. When building a pitch deck for a company, entrepreneurs typically follow these steps:

1. **Describe the mission/goal of the company**. This will help develop a brand and product name.
2. **Develop a product idea**. What are you selling, what service do you provide, how do you make money?
3. **Develop a product plan**. What will it take to build the product? This should include proof of concept, the minimum viable product, the first product that can be sold, production plans, and future products. This will allow you to understand how much money will be required to build the business.
4. **Develop a marketing plan**. Who will buy the product? How much will it cost? How will you market the product? Who will be your first customers? A new company selling a new product is a hard pitch.
5. **Align the management team**. Getting team members who clearly understand what needs to be done and have a proven track record is crucial to the business' success.
6. **Launch the IP strategy or moat**. This allows you to be different from others trying to do a similar thing and can be used to your advantage. This can be intellectual property, marketing deals, trade secrets, or endorsements. What provides you with an advantage or locks others out from competing against you?
7. **Evaluate the financial models** (revenue, funds required). Highlight how and when the company will be profitable. How much will it cost to build the product and run the company? Answers will help determine the value of the company.

When thinking about applying the pitch deck concept to your personal decisions, think of the steps as ways to ensure you are thinking about all aspects of a decision. There are many resources available on ways to develop a pitch deck. The most important aspect is effectively and efficiently telling the story of why this is a good idea.

As you build your pitch deck, you formalize your ideas. It is essential to realize it will take perseverance to succeed. You will meet plenty of doubters along the way. If you struggle in creating a pitch deck, it is a good time to speak with your advisors. Bounce ideas off them to understand the best way to tell your story. Keep in mind this is an iterative process. For the first pass, do the best you can. You will quickly identify strengths and weaknesses in the plan and can start finding ways to fill the gaps and mitigate risks.

Walking the Walk

Remember, where you start is not your destination. It is your starting line. It is time to start your journey and enjoy the ride.

What have you learned from this experience thus far? Always follow your heart and recognize that others may not have the full picture when advising you on certain decisions. In addition, people have biases that may be revealed after asking what you are going to do post-graduation. Do not let that affect your plans.

My mentors from industry emphasized how I should join the workforce. My research advisors told me that going to graduate school would help me develop innovative ideas. Each had their own perspective and agenda that colored their opinions. It is important to be clear when communicating your goals and intentions to others, as it will prevent others from over-influencing your decisions. Figuring out your destination can be correlated to your autonomy of decision-making processes. And once you decide, do not look back.

Chapter Four: Who to Ask for Help?

In this chapter, you will learn:

- How to use the seven degrees of separation concept to your advantage
- How to find advisors with proven track records in a similar field
- How to build out your network so that you are prepared to leverage it during the job search

It is human nature for people to want to help others. You may struggle to take full advantage of formal and informal advising opportunities. This is due to reasons ranging from fear of judgment to determining who to ask or what to ask.

Sometimes you may lack enough activation energy to seek out trusted advisors. It is like getting into exercise. You are reluctant to start, but you are quickly rewarded when you take action. Finding trusted advisors to give you direction can improve your decision-making process. Once you put in the time to develop a network of advisors, it will help develop decision-making skills that will build your foundation for success. Everyone can benefit from a robust set of trusted advisors, whether you are a CEO, a college student, or anyone in between.

The main types of advisors you should focus on learning from are:

- Advisors who have done similar things.

- Advisors who are familiar with and understand your entire situation.
- Advisors with connections to people who are where you want to go, who you want to be.

But first, where do people go for help?

The People Have Spoken

It is a great idea to surround yourself with expert people you trust, individuals who have achieved similar goals. They are your sounding board. Your counsel of advisors will push you out of your comfort zone and provide guidance during the journey. Your advisors may have connections to others who can help you solve problems. The most important thing to remember is to believe in yourself, as you have ultimate control over your decisions. Advisors can provide input, but ultimately you are the one making the final decision. Only you know all the trade-offs and will be the one living with your choices.

Taking advice can greatly impact your life by altering your trajectory in small ways. When it comes to making decisions, who do you go to for advice? After surveying hundreds of individuals about their decision-making processes and support systems for decision-making, some key points stood out.

The top places people go for advice about career, personal matters, and academics:

What places are missing from that list?

In an interview with a young college student, it was clear he knew what he was passionate about: connecting with others and all things related to the circus. After further analysis, it became apparent that his parents were his primary influence. Both were circus performers who were now working in the service industry. For some, this may be a great situation where you find your life passion. For others, it is a situation that shows a heavy influence from parents instead of balanced advice from external advisors. Do not be afraid to leverage resources in the field. Cast a wider net for advisors and do not rely solely on people close to you. Your advisor does not have to be your best friend or family member. Their role is to give you valid information through their personal experiences relevant to what you are trying to achieve.

In life, the primary types of advisors you should look for are:

- Advisors who have done similar things
- Advisors with connections to people who are where you want to be
- Advisors who understand your entire situation

Finding people with connections is key and the easiest of the three types to find, but be sure to look for people you trust.

Fill out a list of advisors you have in each of these categories.

Similar Paths	Other Connections	Understand You

When a college student is deciding whether to pursue an MBA, they can start by surveying friends, family, and professors about the option. Something else they could do to gain clarity during this decision is to talk to managers who have and do not have MBAs to understand their journeys and whether MBAs had helped them in their careers. Find people in the company that have your dream job. Get to know them and how they got where they are. By hearing these firsthand experiences, you can determine whether the MBA helps your career path. You may learn the purpose of obtaining an MBA. Is it used for business acumen? Would you benefit from the prestige of the program? Understand how these factors contribute to your journey.

Thinking in Terms of Degrees of Separation

While building a company, developing an idea, or pursuing a goal, it is essential to go outside the zone of family and friends. It is easier than you may expect to find experts willing to help by using the six degrees of separation phenomenon. You can find mentors and connections by creating a network – and it starts with one person. For example, my sister has a friend whose husband had been an executive for a company in a vertical market. He eventually joined an advisory board for a recent start-up and provided essential insights and guidance for the company.

The bottom line is this: Cast a wide net and use all your connections to build the best group of advisors possible. Keep in mind there are three categories of advisors in business:

- Advisors who have created similar companies
- Advisors with connections to individuals or money
- Advisors who truly understand the technology

Individuals that have created similar companies are the hardest to find. There are people who got lucky. For example, they had the necessary skills, they timed the market or adapted to the market, and they were successful. Perhaps they would struggle to repeat the process. The advisor you want is someone who provides guidance on how to lead your company to success. You need an advisor who is a proven entrepreneur. The real test is whether they can articulate the path forward, quickly understand the value your company provides, comprehend what you are doing, and develop a path to generate revenue.

What are areas of mentorship that are lacking? Write down ideas for how to continue to build your network.

Steps to Take

What are the specific steps you can take to start building your network? Here are some ideas of things to do to get started:

- Connect with old professors and ask if they know anyone in the companies you are interested in, or whether they know of any job opportunities.
- Use LinkedIn to find and message people in companies or on career paths that interest you. Look for someone with similarities to you (e.g., alumni from the same school, same major). This will help with establishing a personal relationship.
- Ask friends, family, people in your social networks if they can connect you with a specific person, role, company, etc.

List your dream team of advisors below. What steps can you take to start populating your advisory board with these individuals or individuals with similar experiences/ expertise?

When to Ask for Help?

You can find mentorships through a number of avenues. Your university can connect you with more experienced individuals. Those types of mentorships are interesting because the selection and pairing process isn't usually standardized. It is hard to have a tailored experience unless the pairing process is focused on a certain outcome. Sometimes mentorships happen organically. Sometimes mentorships can be found for you by a former teacher. Or perhaps a trusted colleague at work can pair you with a mentor.

How do you pick who you are willing to invest in? Based on a variety of interviews, the following factors stood out to make mentors more likely to invest in mentees:

- The mentee has humility and a willingness to learn; someone who will listen to advice.

- The mentee has defined goals and desires — has ambition and direction. The mentee is self-motivated, so the mentor doesn't need to provide the energy.
- The mentee is an honest and genuine person. The mentor doesn't want to waste their time.

Many people are surprised at the willingness of others to serve as mentors, especially when so many successful people are extremely busy and occupied with a million other things piling up on their plate. Never underestimate how a genuine desire to learn and improve can lead you to mentors who are willing to take the time to help.

When I was employed in my first internship, I was initially hesitant to reach out to more senior staff for fear of bothering them or wasting their time. I soon realized many people get satisfaction from mentoring others, especially if they see their younger self in you. Some mentors may serve as a resource. With others, you may develop a deeper connection that will help to guide your path forward.

Boards for Support

As you begin to collect your trusted advisors along the journey, think of them as your board of advisors. This is similar to a board of advisors that helps influence decision-making at large corporations. Your advisors are invested in your success, which means you can ask them for their perspectives at any time. You can add or replace members on your advisory board depending on what you and your company need. Expect these individuals to challenge you and push you to consider the entire picture.

Who is on your board of advisors? Think of mentors, role models, and key influencers in your life who you go to for help.

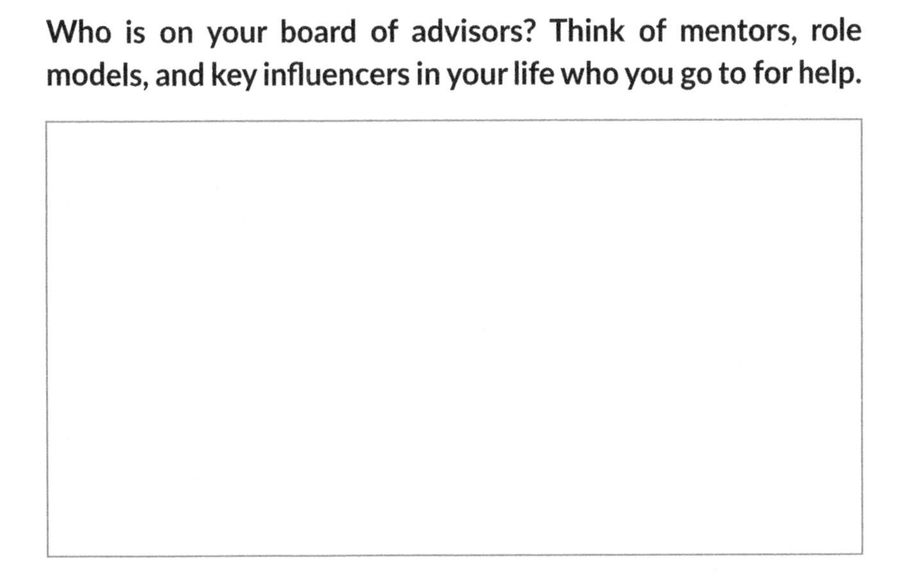

Now comes the hard part. You have a great advisory board, and they provide a wealth of advice. How will you use this advice to drive your decision process? You do not have to meet regularly with them, but they are there when you need them. These boards are trusted people in your life, and their advice should be weighted more heavily than the information you gather from random sources.

In some cases, advisors are useful in their ability to steer you away from bad decisions and wrong directions. For people who like to take risks, advisors can warn against bad decisions or help slow the decision-making process enough for you to think through risky actions thoroughly.

Influence vs. Control

With advisors contributing to your decisions, it is important to differentiate between influence and control to ensure that you stay the navigator on your journey. Influence is when advisors give advice and suggestions that provide fair trade-offs and are ultimately in your best interest. Control is when advisors take charge with ultimatums or simply tell you what to do. They should provide their insights and leave the final decision-making to you. What happens when you have an advisor that seems to have every answer and expects you to follow exactly what they say — their way or the highway? The simple answer is to take their advice into account, but distance yourself so you can stay in control of your decision-making process.

The diagram below walks you through how to think about receiving advice from various sources. It is important to consider the potential bias of the advisor and filter it accordingly.

Don't Forget to Use Your Backpack

Keep in mind that this whole time you have been collecting experiences in your backpack. Let this help guide you in your mentor selection and decision-making. Instead of finding a doctor and asking whether or not you should pursue that field, draw on things you have done or learned. For example, my boss said I was good at listening to the needs of customers, so I could apply this skill to be a doctor. I went on a mission trip, and we helped children with illnesses. During the trip, one of the doctors told me how, for him, taking care of people in need was far more gratifying than taking care of patients back home. Maybe you shadowed a doctor and enjoyed the entire experience. This experience helps inform your decision more than asking a doctor whether you should go to medical school.

Chapter Five: Adjust Your Speed

In this chapter, you will learn:

- Reach out to companies and people with a perspective on the "riskiness" of the opportunity
- What risk is perceived, and what is real?
- What are drivers to apply to companies vs. a startup vs. starting your own company?
- Get in touch with how comfortable and interested you are in risk when seeking opportunities

Adjusting your speed is knowing when to accelerate to your destination, when to slow down, and when to pivot and change your direction. It is critical to realize when an opportunity is knocking and when it's time to alter your route. For each of these decision points, there is some amount of risk that needs to be understood and addressed. The question is: Can you tip the odds in your favor when risk-taking? Can you mitigate the risk by having a plan B? Can your plan B break the risk into smaller, manageable chunks that can be addressed? Addressing these points means that you will land on your feet even if it turns out to be a bad decision.

For successful entrepreneurs, business people, and investors, risk is an inherent part of the journey to success. It is important to understand how to evaluate risk and mitigate what you can to set yourself up for best-possible-scenario outcomes at every point along your journey.

Risky Business

Risk-taking is a willingness to take risky action in the hope of a desired result.

Some people view risks as taking a chance with a low probability of success. For example, imagine putting your entire life savings into Bitcoin with an opportunity to make a massive profit. Other people view risk in a different light. It allows them to be more comfortable with risk. For example, imagine putting a portion of your funds into Bitcoin, knowing that if the value skyrockets, as it did in early 2018, the profit will help launch your next great idea. Alternately, if the value plummets, as it did in late 2018, it will have no impact on your lifestyle.

The question is: Are there ways to tip the odds in your favor when risk-taking?

We interviewed a wide range of people, and a few interesting ideas started to crystalize. What seemed to be very bold and risky moves from an outsider (such as leaving a great corporate job to venture out and start a company), were in fact well thought out plans that focused on mitigating risk and ensuring a successful outcome.

The first step is understanding what is at risk. Then you can develop a mitigation strategy. Risks come in many forms — identify the types of risks you will face before developing your mitigation strategy.

Types of risk:

Financial — Placing financial stability at risk. Loss of savings, income, or bankruptcy.

Relationship – Making decisions that impact family and friends. For example, moving away may upset family and friends.

Core beliefs – Working in an industry that is contrary to your principles or goals. For example, "I am passionate about environmentalism and sustainability, but the company I work for is dumping trash in an illegal dumping zone even though I have confronted them about the matter."

Safety – Losing focus on your wellbeing. Are you putting your physical or mental health at risk?

Mitigating Risk

Below are some steps to take when evaluating different decisions and their relative riskiness:

1. **List the Risk:** List the risks that may result from your decision. Once you have a list, you can start to develop a mitigation strategy.
2. **Rank the Risks:** Reorder the risks and rank them, first to last, from the biggest risk to the smallest risk.
3. **Worst Case:** Identify the worst consequence, starting with the biggest risk. The goal is to work toward the best outcome but ensure the worst outcome is manageable.
4. **Mitigation:** Brainstorm ways to mitigate each risk – speak with advisors about the risks and possible mitigation strategies. Your risk mitigation strategy is the key to repeatable success in decision-making

The more you can mitigate the risk, the better chance you have for success. It is important to realize that taking risks is acceptable. You want to ensure the outcomes are manageable. What is manageable will differ for everyone. Some people will think investing their 401k to start a business is a manageable risk. Others will view that as an unacceptable risk. It all depends on your age, stage of life, and psychological mindset.

Being an entrepreneur requires some risk-taking. Entrepreneurs are willing to take risks because they believe in their brand and have mitigated their risks.

Consider this example. I am trying to determine if now is the right time to branch out and start my own law practice. Now, I apply the four-step risk mitigation plan:

1. My biggest risk is not being able to get clients. This would lead to no income, which means, based on my business and living expenses, my finances will last six months.

   Worst Case (Step 3): This would be hard to take, but I could find another firm to hire me full-time. It may require a move as the fallback.

   Mitigation (Step 4):

   - Build up more considerable savings to provide another six months of funds.
   - Partner with another lawyer to consolidate costs.
   - Investigate techniques that allow me to gain clients via mailings or targeted ads. After speaking with an advisor who started his own firm, I had a list of ways to gain new clients. He suggested developing my marketing approach before starting the firm, so I have clients from day one.
   - Investigate buying an existing law practice. An old law professor advised me to reach out to alumni in their

late 60's to see whether any are interested in taking on a lawyer to buy out the firm.

2. My girlfriend is nervous I will not be able to generate my current income level for several years, which means a lifestyle change for us both.

   Worst Case (Step 3): This could cause a break-up, which would be terribly painful. It would take a while to move on emotionally. But I am sure I will meet other great people that would be more supportive.

   Mitigation (Step 4)

   - Talk things over with her about how I am mitigating risks. Explain that no matter what happens, we will be OK. My law professor thinks that if my girlfriend is not going to be supportive, then there may be a bigger issue at play. He says when things get difficult, you discover who your true friends are and who is along for fun. Of course, this is just one perspective.
   - Talk about lifestyle and make sure everyone considers the risks that are acceptable and what would be considered too risky.
   - Make sure you have a supportive group of friends as you make the difficult transition to starting your own firm.

3. I can't afford an office in the city close to where I live, so I will need to commute to work outside of the city.

   Worst Case (Step 3): I cannot afford to live in the city or take time for a long commute to the suburbs. I must move the business out of the city and can commute in to meet clients when I am able to get clients in the city.

Mitigation (Step 4):

- Investigate whether moving closer to the office will make the transition easier
- Look at ways to utilize the commute time to be productive
- Work from home unless I have clients

Rank the listed risks below, mapping out the worst-case scenario and how you could mitigate risk during the process.

List Risks:

-
-
-
-

Rank Risks:

1.

Worst case:

Mitigation:

2.

Worst case:

Mitigation:

3.

Worst case:

Mitigation:

4.

Worst case:

Mitigation:

5.

Worst case:

Mitigation:

Smart Partnerships

You are never expected to have all the skills and know-how to do every task needed. When thinking about risk, something to consider is how you are spending your time. Sometimes you need to ask yourself whether a partner can help get the job done. Even if you have the skills to complete a task, are there ways to outsource some of the work so that you can spend your time solving problems that only you can solve. This helps to mitigate risks as you can make sure all steps are handled with excellence. It also ensures you have the brain capacity to think about bigger-picture tasks and decisions.

Smart partnerships can also be thought of in terms of how you organize your team or company. Are you able to hire individuals who help cover blind spots you may have? Or could you work with partners who can bolster specific skills in a specific industry? By thinking strategically about what skill sets you surround yourself with, you are taking steps to mitigate the risk of failure.

Entrepreneurial Mindset

When thinking about job opportunities, there are many risk factors to consider. One way of mitigating risk in larger decisions is by taking smaller opportunities to learn what you like and don't like. This is where internships, part-time jobs, and volunteer opportunities can help to crystalize what you like and don't like in a role, company, or opportunity. That way, when you start to make full-time or career-changing decisions, you are tipping the odds in your favor to help set you up for success.

Are you unsure if you want to start your own company or work at a larger company? Try working at a large company.

Take advantage of time in college when you are able to explore via internships, research experiences, and volunteer opportunities. When it is time to decide whether to start a company or work for a larger company, you will have more clarity about what you are looking for to set yourself up for future success.

Improving Your Odds

Are there ways to improve your odds during risk-taking? How do you take risks in a controlled way? Before taking risks, you should understand a few key factors that can help improve your odds:

1. Do you have the skills in your backpack to succeed?
2. Do you have a safety net?
3. Do you have a plan B if things don't work out?
4. What is the worst possible outcome?
5. Are you prepared for that worst possible outcome?
6. What other options are available to you?

These are critical factors that apply to companies that are risk-takers, e.g., casinos. Casinos take risks in a controlled way. If they run into problems, they can change the rules. That is exactly what happened after a casino caught a group of MIT students counting cards. Most of us are not in a position to change the rules like casinos, but our ability to control or mitigate risk is possible. The most successful risk-takers are the repeaters, people who do things repeatedly and learn from each experience. It appears to be risk-taking, but they have a solid plan before they undertake the risk. Understand that you can do your best to mitigate risk, but often, there will be circumstances beyond your control. By going through the process of risk mitigation for large and small decisions, you will be better prepared for the unexpected.

Chapter Six: Dealing with Roadblocks

In this chapter, you will learn:

- How to consider failures as an opportunity to learn and grow
- How to know when to pivot
- How to bounce back from rejections or lack of response
- Why "adapt", "adjust", and "overcome", are your new go-to words

There are inevitably going to be times that try your spirit and make you question your current route. Journeys are filled with potholes, bumpy roads, and unexpected situations that leave you needing a tow truck or a therapy session. How can you learn to deal with problems and failures in a positive way? The answer lies in your perception of the situation – how you choose to deal with it.

If you look up inspirational quotes about failure, you will see a near infinite number that convey the idea that failure makes you stronger and wiser. The key is how you react to the situation and adjust your plan moving forward.

During your career journey, you likely will receive more rejections than acceptances. Many individuals we interviewed mentioned it took them 40+ rejections to get one acceptance, which turned out to be their dream job! This indicates that both luck and probability enter into the equation of opportunity. The idea is to transform failures into learning opportunities and perhaps a sign that it is time to pivot.

Processing Failure

Sometimes not getting the grant you applied for, the funding you pitched hard for, or the job you put everything into but didn't get can be low points in your journey. No one likes feeling as though your hard work is not paying off. Bluntly stated: Sometimes you need to process the bad. Don't pity yourself; process the feelings and use that energy to drive you forward. Sometimes it takes time to look back and understand the role certain rejections or unexpected turns played in your life.

Everyone processes information differently. It is important to think critically and uncouple emotion from difficult situations. This is helpful when identifying the difference between perceived failure vs. actual failure. Many individuals tend to be hard on themselves when decision making and goal setting. This causes situations where you feel as though you are facing barriers. Instead, you should be thinking about how to pivot to make sure it doesn't happen again. An example of this is when a funding source falls through or when you fail a big exam. Instead of feeling sorry for yourself, think about what needs to change to enable yourself to reach the goal next time. Is there a different way you should be pitching your company or studying for the exam? How can you use your skills, experiences, and advisors to your advantage to help set yourself up for success? Take a moment to focus on the big-picture goal you are working towards, and recenter yourself.

Learn and Grow

It is as important to learn from your successes as it is from your failures. In fact, failures make for the best growing experiences. After learning from the *Recalculating for Entrepreneurs* method to make decisions and set goals, you will realize that speed bumps are essential points along the journey for evaluating your progress. Sometimes setbacks are signals that help us pivot in the right direction. Other times, they serve as reflection points to help you understand the key information you need to make the best decision in the least amount of time. There are other times where road bumps serve as a reset point for re-evaluating what your goals are.

This exercise will help you think about your road bumps from a growth mindset. **Fill out the chart below to better understand how specific road bumps you encountered help guide you in the right direction. Use our initial examples as reference**.

Example of road bump/failure	What was the key piece of information (make or break)	I learned that...	So, I pivoted and...
We said we would be able to license a product to manufacturers, but they were not interested in changing their business model	We believed manufacturers would embrace a DTC sales model based on our technology	Manufacturers don't want to change their current business models	Launched the product direct to consumer through our website
Failed my physics exam	I studied the homework, but none of that was on the exam	I needed to focus on understanding the core concepts so that I can solve all types of problems (not just ones I am familiar with)	Went to office hours every week and practiced problems without solution guides next to me

Mistakes happen. Success depends on not making the same mistake repeatedly. Processing road bumps helps encourage us to learn from our experiences, think critically about when to pivot, and what needs to happen to continue moving in the right direction.

How to Know When to Pivot

During your journey, there are going to be times when road bumps or potholes are reflection points for you to think about how things are going. They are times to consider whether you want to change the direction in which you are going. Sometimes unexpected outcomes are the foundation for something new and great to develop. Other times, unexpected outcomes may totally derail your plan and leave you feeling discouraged and unsure about whether to abandon the journey or continue moving forward. Failure has a positive side if you can learn from it. The concept of fail-fast was based on the notion that it is better to cut your losses than continue to invest time and someone else's money in an idea that has a low chance of success. The concept of fail-fast works best when there is a well-thought-out plan on how to ensure success and mitigate risk. Then, it is easy to realize the endeavor is headed for failure and needs to be stopped.

So how do you know when to pivot? One way is to be vigilant for a better opportunity than you currently have and see that as a moment to pivot. This approach works sometimes. Our goal is to make the pivot end in a positive outcome. To achieve this, you need to understand your current situation. Ask yourself what is working and not working for you. Once you understand your current situation, you can compare it to a new opportunity to determine if it makes sense for you to pivot. You need to quickly assess how your strengths and weakness align with the new opportunity. When you make the comparison, it may take some time to feel comfortable to pivot. It is fine to start slowly. As you develop the skills to make the comparison, it will become easier and faster.

Each time you pivot, you need to document the driving forces and the outcome. You want to make sure you understand what leads to good outcomes and ways to avoid repeating mistakes. From my own observation, people tend to celebrate successful outcomes without understanding what caused the success. When an unsuccessful outcome occurs, we tend to push them aside and regroup. In both cases, you need to analyze your journal to understand what decision indicators led to successful outcomes and what decision indicators led to poor outcomes. By doing this, you are developing a knowledge base that will lead to repeatable successful outcomes. Each time you pivot, it will take you less time to realize if it makes sense to do so. Remember, the goal of the pivot is to reach your destination more quickly. With this goal in mind, pivots are worth trying if we believe they will help us reach our destination or gain a life skill/experience as part of our journey.

Key Signals

Look for key signals that indicate it may be time to pivot your plan, destination, or approach:

- Stuck at a certain level (not able to accelerate promotions)
- Interested in a new area/type of work
- Looking to change locations
- Repeating the same mistake
- You keep getting the same unwanted outcome

- You are unhappy the majority of the time with how things are going

The ultimate test of your decision-making ability is when things are not going as planned and you are under pressure to turn things around quickly. Some of your supporters may scrutinize your decisions. When things start to go in the wrong direction, the first question you need to ask yourself is: What has changed? Is this something that is within your control to change? If you feel like nothing has changed and all indicators continue to show you are on the right path, then staying the course may be the best course of action.

How do you know if you are on the right path? If you are working with a recruiter and they are happy with your resume, requested salary range, and the number of job prospects who have shown interest is reasonable, you are probably on the right path. It may take a few non-offers before you find your dream job, but you have an advisor helping to guide you through the process. On the other hand, if the recruiter is saying your salary range is unrealistic for your experience level, it could be an indicator that you may need to rethink your strategy for the job you are seeking.

However, if you are starting to get indicators that there is a bigger problem at hand, it's time to do a quick re-assessment and a potential recalculating. If the salary range is out of line, a move you can make is to better highlight your skills in the domain you are targeting. Then they can evaluate you based on capabilities you can contribute instead of years of experience. Use your resume creatively to showcase your value and convince the employer you are the right person for the job. It is your time to shine, but you need to take action to make it happen.

This is just an example of when to stay or pivot. There will be times when the data clearly indicates it is time to take a different approach. When that happens, step back and focus on skills and experiences in your backpack.

Rejection is Tough

With rejections, there are two paths that can commonly happen:

1. I'm on the right path, and the rejection doesn't provide enough information to make an immediate decision.

2. The rejection indicates you are not interpreting or decoding the information the same way (as your "rejector") and that you need to pivot.

Case #1 suggests you continue down the same path—but first, do some recalculating. If you get a rejection and you know you are on the right path, how do you learn from the feedback? This is very tricky, especially as an entrepreneur. Most of the feedback you are likely to receive about ideas, proposals, and plans will be negative. It may make you uncomfortable when you receive feedback that the business will fail, no one will buy that, etc. Consider the source of the feedback. The negative comments may come from less skilled or experienced people in what you are trying to achieve. The cautionary advice is not as helpful and, perhaps, misleading.

Therefore, it is crucial to speak with advisors who have been successful in a similar field. They can provide accurate information that will help you evaluate the rejection and whether something needs to change. It is essential to understand the data points you are using to validate that you are on the right path. Conversely, examine the information that is driving your rejection. For every business I started, half the people I spoke with told me it wasn't going to be successful. Needless to say, it was largely all talk with very little actionable advice.

Consider case #2, in which the feedback for the rejection are reasons you had not considered or even underestimated. In this case, you will need to determine the action required to get around the rejection. For example, we tried to license our technology to several companies that all had some interest, but none were willing to close a deal with us. The technology was sound, but it didn't fit their marketing strategy. After several rejections, we realized we needed to modify our business plan and figure out how to sell directly to the consumer.

This point is the true test of your decision-making. There is an increased time constraint, and you are relying more on your scaffolding to understand what you need to change. This is when you start thinking about other options. What could you have done differently? Who do you need to work with to help solve the problem? This needs to be supported by a formal method; otherwise, there is nothing to be done to make it repeatable. Your scaffolding allows you to make the best decision based on your time constraints. Once your decision is made, it is important to go back, evaluate, and make sure you interpreted the information correctly.

Bounce Back

Resiliency is the ability to deal with setbacks and continue to move forward. Perseverance is moving forward when things get tough. They are similar. The only difference is perseverance doesn't consider adapting while resiliency does. Perseverance is sticking with it. Resiliency is bouncing back.

The roles of perseverance and resilience are worth exploring. They can be used to mitigate the impact when dealing with roadblocks. Perseverance enables you to continue to execute your plan while there are roadblocks. Resiliency serves you when things don't go your way, and you must quickly adjust your plan based on roadblocks.

We all deal with rejections that feel difficult to bounce back from. For example:

- Your "in-the-bag" job has fallen through
- Your employer needs to reduce staff, so they decided to let you go
- Your lead investor has lost interest in continuing to fund your effort
- Your boss has turned down your request to transfer to a different division
- No one is interested in providing seed money for your company to get it off the ground

When one or a series of roadblocks are encountered during your journey, it is crucial to know when to act and when to stay on course. This is where an understanding of the information that was used in the initial decision will need to be evaluated (what we like to call your scaffolding). You can quickly determine if one of the key decision points has changed or not. It helps you feel confident about whether the roadblock was caused by a miscalculation or change of circumstances. Because you typically make decisions in a time-constrained environment, this point of reflection can help you better understand how to optimize decision-making in the future. Do you need more time or more information? Should you trust your gut?

Using Your Backpack

When things are not going as planned, and you may feel the urge to quit, that is the time to lean on your backpack and advisors. The first step is to review what is in your backpack with a fresh set of eyes. It may be worth doing a quick re-read of the chapter so that you can update the information in your backpack. Look for any experience you can leverage to help develop a new plan of attack or a pivot in direction to get around the roadblock. Use this re-evaluation to refresh your memory and see if you have family or friends in the field who can help you get an introduction. It may be the case where you find similar problems that appeared in your journal before, and they will provide inspiration on how to navigate around the problem.

Another area to investigate is your scaffolding to see what has changed. Then talk with your advisors about ways to deal with the changes you have identified. When speaking with your advisors, discuss your situation and brainstorm potential ways to navigate around issues. If your current advisors can't help, see if they know of someone who can. Another approach is to talk with friends and co-workers to see if they can introduce you to someone they know who has gone through a similar problem. You want to leverage every relationship you have to find potential solutions quickly. This will enable you to identify your best option and then act.

There comes the point when you need to decide and act. Understand the consequences of your decisions and accept them. We sometimes inflate the gravity of decision-making. Most decisions aren't fatal. It is the chain of bad decisions that will hurt you. Keep a keen perspective on things and lean on your backpack and advisors during the journey.

Go-To Words

You are going to end up encountering many road bumps and potholes during your journey. Adapt, adjust, and overcome are words that help keep you aware of signals for change and what you can do about it. There are resources available to you that help you adapt, adjust, and overcome anything that comes your way.

Adapt – Be willing to assess your situation from an honest viewpoint and modify your path, always trying to leverage your backpack to make the journey easier. You don't need to take the hardest path to your destination. You want to find a balanced path, focusing on working smarter, not harder.

Adjust – This requires some more complex decisions about changing route during your journey. Do you need to acquire additional tools to succeed? Has the timing for your great idea passed (so it is time to let go of the idea and move on)? Think about what needs to change to enable you to reach your goals.

Overcome – Leverage your backpack and experience to find another way to your destination. Look for shortcuts you may have overlooked. You may need to pivot and take a detour to get to your destination. You may need to develop a plan to reach your destination, and leverage advisors to help pull the plan together.

These words help overcome roadblocks and potholes along your journey, however big or small those may be. While "adapt" focuses on changes you need to be ready for during your journey, "adjust" requires harder decisions. While adapting and overcoming help navigate the small bumps or changes, it is important to be aware of potential points when you must recalculate. Make the necessary decisions and hold onto your passion and strength to power on and reach your destination.

Chapter Seven: Active Thinking Along the Route

In this chapter, you will learn:

- How to optimize your decision making
- How to use benchmarking to your advantage
- How to maintain your scaffolding during the good and the bad
- How to embrace opportunity as it comes

Detours Ahead

Have you ever started on a path with a specific plan and goal in mind, only to have everything go wrong and your plan (as well as a bit of pride you may have had) is thrown out the window? Well, it happens to all of us. What if there was a way to evaluate your path before you got to the point of chaos and failure?

Active thinking gives you the ability to take things — opportunities, information, decisions — as they come. It helps you evaluate based on where you are at that given moment and where you want to go in the future. It supports better decision-making with less agonizing about the decision process. Detours happen all the time. You can either curse the detour for disrupting your journey or use it as an opportunity to explore a new path you might not have taken otherwise. In the moment when you need to decide whether to turn, how do you know if you are going to end up in the right direction?

During your decision-making journey, there will be some wrong turns and unexpected outcomes which may test your resolve to keep pushing forward. A wrong turn may also lead to a serendipitous outcome that alters your priorities and leads to recalculating your route.

Much of this book focuses on tools and techniques to formalize your active thinking skills. *Recalculating for Entrepreneurs'* goal is to help you make better decisions during your journey and to give you the tools to overcome any obstacles in your way. Ultimately, this process helps to train your intuition to align with your decision-making. If this means learning through a few long, drawn-out decisions, then so be it. .

Gaining Speed

Gaining speed refers to our ability to make quality decisions quickly. Gaining speed in making quality decisions is a skill that you will continue to refine during your journey. As your journey progresses, decisions should change from all-encompassing (requiring all your time and energy) to becoming a natural intuition that flows throughout your journey. You have been building your scaffolding over the past five chapters through points of reflection that help to keep you on track for your decision-making. This chapter focuses on how to leverage the scaffolding that supports you on your destination with the current state of your backpack (skills/experiences) and new opportunities.

Scaffolding is a tool that will constantly support you as you make decisions. This applies to big and small decisions and to decisions you can make quickly vs. draw out. Eventually, you develop an intuition that helps guide your decision-making as you subconsciously process the factors that affect your scaffolding. This helps to remove the emotion from decision-making that may get in the way of your seeing clearly.

Scaffolding helps you utilize the skills and tools in your backpack successfully. Over time, it becomes second nature. It is like the intuition of fighter pilots. They intuitively ask themselves, "Am I in a good position or bad position? What do I need to do next?" The faster you make those decisions, the more likely you are to return home. You are building skills to leverage over your lifetime. The first time you must make a huge decision, it may seem like a lengthier process. But you are building a foundation for future decisions to be made more efficiently.

The following chart will help you keep track of what worked and what didn't work during key decision points. What was the key piece of information you needed to make the call? Think about what could have been done to optimize the speed of the decision.

Decision	What went well	What didn't go well	What could have been done to optimize the decision speed?
Example: To reject my graduate school offer	I was able to learn about both industry and grad school and connect with people in the field	Felt frustrated when the professor I was interested in was not responding, and I felt unsure whether to accept a position	Picked up on the signals earlier that the position I wanted wasn't going to work out (otherwise, it would have been a quicker response)

As you begin to speed up your decision-making process, there is a chance you could make the "wrong decision." Wrong turns can lead to unexpected destinations that add to your life experiences. Don't live in fear of mistakes. Instead, embrace what comes your way and know that you can always regain control and recalculate.

Monkey See

Part of the process of learning from your decisions is understanding that you can learn from others' experiences too. If you are exploring what companies you are interested in, talk with your friends who are working at other companies with the goal of learning from their experiences. You may be able to gain clarity about a route you would be interested in. If you are considering creating a start-up, talk to other co-founders to see what key pieces of information dictated their journey. And see if there are insights you can gain for your own backpack. Keep in mind this works better with more information gained about others' journeys. You can understand the reality of their assumptions and the decision they faced. That way, you can better filter through what is relevant.

Don't be afraid to share your experiences. By being open to sharing, others may be more willing to share what is in their backpacks so you can learn from them. A friend of mine worked at a company and wasn't enjoying the project they were on. Instead of communicating feelings and ideas with management, they ended up slacking off to the point where they were fired. Everyone can learn from this situation. It is important to monitor your feelings and attitudes and leverage your network of advisors to ensure you are in a good situation. All companies want employees to be engaged and know that employees are putting in their best work.

There are many situations you don't need to experience personally before adding them to your backpack. One area in which you can learn from others' experiences is management styles. At some point in your career, you will have a difficult manager. Instead of complaining, use the time to figure out how to handle the situation. It is a perfect opportunity to speak with your mentors about how they would handle issues with that manager. Record this information and advice in your journal for future reference.

Think about an experience someone in your inner circle had that was a relevant data point for you along your journey. Map out how this knowledge impacted your backpack below (see example).

Situation	I learned that	Therefore
I was considering whether to go to graduate school. My brother was currently studying to get his PhD.	Grad school was a really difficult journey and worth it if the job I want requires this degree or if it is a life-long goal.	I was able to learn that the positions I was interested in did not require a PhD. Therefore, I could start making more money at an earlier point of my life.

Should I Stay, or Should I Go?

When we talk about active thinking, there is a hierarchy of change:

- Your route can change often
- Your destination should change infrequently
- Your goals should be stable

In fact, if you feel a significant change to your destination or goal is required, it is best to rebuild your scaffolding. This helps you understand how the changes align with your resources and skills. Examine the constraints that are apparent to help you arrive at your destination and achieve your goals. When we talk about day-to-day and week-to-week active thinking, focus on: "What new data is available that has an impact on my destination?"

Let's dive into this concept more deeply with an example: Suppose several of your co-workers are looking to get a higher salary at other companies. This data point should prompt the following questions:

- Is my compensation at a comparable level?
- Should I go on a few interviews to determine my worth?
- Can I check a pay scale site online to compare my pay with market salaries?

Consider another example: Suppose you are 35 years old and have not found the person you want to spend the rest of your life with and raise a family. Do you need to change some of your constraints, destination, or goals? This may require a fresh examination of the scaffolding that is driving your decision-making. Active thinking allows you to be vigilant about what is happening around you that could impact your direction. Active thinking prevents you from becoming hyper-focused on arriving at your destination. It pushes you to be more aware of potential shortcuts and pivots that will lead to a more enjoyable journey and ultimately a better outcome.

There may be other cases where something outside of your control disrupts your scaffolding and plan. An example of this is when working from home became the norm for many during the COVID-19 pandemic in early 2020. It forced everyone to embrace meeting virtually, which provided a new way to interact with customers without traveling. It allowed for new players to disrupt the market since the cost to set up a meeting was so low. This leveled the playing field for small businesses to present their products to new customers while bypassing the previous obstacle of arranging in-person meetings. It was transformational for any startup, as it provided a way to interact with customers directly. In 2010, it could have taken a month to arrange a meeting with a potential customer. That time is in addition to the cost of travel to the potential clients' facility and the loss of three days of work for a single interaction. The new model enables arranging a 30-minute introductory meeting and, if there is interest, quickly arrange a follow-up meeting within a week. The norm of virtual meetings requires a complete change in how businesses interact with potential customers and greatly reduces the cost of sales.

There will be times where you question if you are in the right role. It is crucial to think about the big picture and what is driving your uncertainty. If you are thinking about leaving a company, why are you making the move? Money, location, title? Think about whether this is a step towards your goals compared to your present role. Sometimes it takes a job change to move you to a higher salary or promoted position. Other times, there may be benefits to stay or transfer to a different role in the same company.

The flow chart below illustrates steps to help you actively think about the best decision for you to make. Reflect on how this flowchart can be modified to fit your current situation.

ACTIVE THINKING

Sunk Cost

At some point, we all face the following problem: We invest a lot of time and energy in a decision to assure a successful outcome. No matter what the data is telling us or advice from advisors, we want to ignore the information and focus on reaching a successful outcome.

This is the entrepreneur's dilemma: Do you follow your instincts and continue to push forward or cut your losses? It could be the case that your network of advisors is pushing you away from a specific outcome or goal. At what point do you consider it a sunk cost and move on, or put all your power into the decision until the final outcome?

When considering whether your effort is a sunk cost or something worth pushing forward, there are many factors to ponder. It may be the case that you are so focused on the goal, you are not articulating the situation well for others to understand. It could also be that you are seeing something that others are missing. Perhaps you are misinterpreting the information or have become overly biased.

For one of my companies, my investors told me we are running out of runway (a nice way of saying you don't have the funding to pull this off). I was very close to closing a major deal that would get everything back on track. I continued to ignore the runway issue and focused on closing the deal. Eventually, I was able to close it and came to the board feeling pumped up for pulling off the impossible. Unfortunately, I presented the deal to my board, and one of the board members had an issue. As part of the license deal, the licensee would provide the company with a $500,000 influx of cash in the form of a loan. This would allow us to continue operations with our requiring additional capital. The board member was against this because he felt the board/investors could be stuck paying back the loan if the product failed. I was so upset. Here I had pulled off a miracle, and my investors were against the deal.

I have spent a lot of time thinking about this encounter and realized what the issue was. We were looking at the data differently. We were not working to solve a problem but to prove each of us was right. To make matters worse, the board had to come up with $500,000 to position the company for sale. The correct action should have been to make the board aware of the negotiation and their direction so I could explain why this was the best outcome for everyone. I got so caught up in closing the deal, and I forgot to inform everyone else and get them on board and excited about it. When I told the company the board didn't approve the deal, it created a situation where the company lost faith in our board. It was not a pleasant exchange. Another issue at play here was that all parties needed to look at the data, express their opinions based on the information available, and leave emotion out of the decision-making.

When you believe strongly in a position, it is worth looking to ensure the data in your scaffolding supports your position while also informing your doubters to help them understand the full situation. This will help remove the emotion and focus everyone on trying to achieve the best outcome together.

Speak Now

A mentor of mine in college interned every summer with the same company. She ended up accepting a full-time offer with them. She loved the company culture but was hesitant about her work and the impact she felt she was making. She seemed enthusiastic about her experience and was content with her role.

A year later, when talking to my mentor, she mentioned that she was thinking of quitting. I immediately had so many questions. Did something happen? Had she been thinking about quitting for a while? She explained that she had been mildly unhappy for a couple of months, so she wanted a change. As I began to dig deeper into this problem, I found out that she had been unhappy, but her manager had no idea. She had never informed anyone about her concerns. She hadn't talked to people in other departments to see if she would like that work more. In her head, it was a "stay or go" decision.

This is an example of the importance of active thinking. When little warning signs go off in your head, don't ignore them until the situation reaches the point of an all-or-nothing decision. Those feeling are guides to help you realign and readjust with your goals. You have networks of people available to help you, and all you must do is ask.

After All is Said and Done

Remember that recalculating is a process, and its goal is to help you make better decisions in less time. Celebrate your successes, learn from others, track your skills in your backpack, and log your experiences in your journal. It is all about the journey, and part of your journey is continuing to grow and move towards your goals. Don't expect everything to always turn out perfectly. But know that *Recalculating for Entrepreneurs* is there to help you along the way. You are the CEO, and this is your journey.

Made in the USA
Las Vegas, NV
03 February 2023

66808026R00057